A Book About Planets and Stars

*A revised and expanded version
of A BOOK ABOUT PLANETS*

by Betty Polisar Reigot

SCHOLASTIC INC.

New York Toronto London Auckland Sydney

For Jeanie, Paula, and Jonathan

Acknowledgments

*For their help in offering information and research materials,
thanks to the National Aeronautics and Space Administration
and to the University of North Carolina Library of Physics,
Mathematics and Astronomy, for making available the most recent data
in the ongoing scientific exploration of the universe.*

ISBN 0-590-40593-4

12 11 10 9 8 7 6 5   0 1 2 3/9

Printed in the U.S.A.   08
First Scholastic printing, September 1988

CONTENTS

INTRODUCTION

This book is about two parts of the universe we can see just standing outdoors on a clear night and looking up at the sky — the stars and planets.

Out in space, there are millions of stars. Scientists believe that planets go around them. The sun is one of those stars. Earth is one of the planets that goes around the sun.

Stars, like our sun, shine with their own light. Planets have no light of their own. They are lit by the light that falls on them from their star.

No one on Earth has yet been to other planets. But we have many ways of learning about them and the rest of the universe:

- Telescopes and computers are among the many special instruments that help us find out what happens in space.

- Space shuttles carry travelers beyond Earth, where they get firsthand information about life in space. In 1987, an astronaut from the Soviet Union returned to Earth after almost one year in space. It may be possible to live in space for many years — perhaps a lifetime.

- Satellites brought into space by the shuttle orbit around our planet for years, sending new data back to Earth all the time.

- Space probes, loaded with instruments, are rocketed into space. They go farthest away, picking up signals about our universe that tell us what may be out there.

Instruments and spacecraft help us find out what may have happened millions and billions of years ago in outer space, billions and trillions of kilometers away. Astronomers and other scientists can figure out when and where something may happen in space in the future. Best of all, they gradually learn how and why things happen as they do in our universe.

We are finding out so much so fast that by the time you finish reading this book, there will be more information to write about! But some of what we already know is a good place to start.

We know that our big Earth is like a tiny speck in space.

THE SOLAR SYSTEM

Earth is one of nine known planets that go around our star, the sun. Other objects go around the sun, too — large chunks of rocks called asteroids, balls of ice called comets, and dust particles. All of these belong to our solar system.

Our solar system is in the Milky Way galaxy. There are millions of other systems in this galaxy. The Milky Way galaxy is part of the universe.

From Earth, the other planets look flat. But they are really shaped more like balls.

Planets move in two ways. Every planet turns around and around like a spinning top. This movement is called rotating.

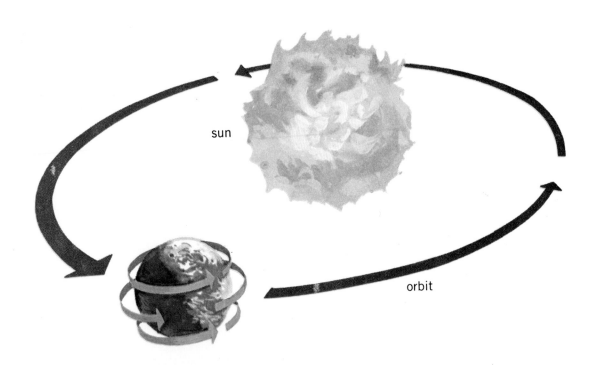

sun

orbit

As each planet rotates, it also follows a path around the sun. The path is called an orbit. We say the planet orbits (revolves around) the sun.

Something else makes our solar system work the way it does. It is a force called gravity.

Gravity — the greatest force of all

When you hold a pencil in your hand and let it go, it falls to the ground. Why doesn't it float in the air?

A great scientist, Albert Einstein, explained why. Everything is made up of matter. The amount of matter an object has is called its mass. Some objects have great mass. Some have little. In space objects with great mass pull other objects to them. That pull is a force called gravity.

Because Earth's mass is great, its pull of gravity — or gravitational [GRAV-it-TAY-shun-ul] force — is also great. It pulls the pencil toward Earth's center and keeps it from floating in air. Gravity keeps us from floating in air, too.

The sun

The sun, which is a million times larger than Earth, contains an enormous amount of matter. Its mass is far greater than Earth's.

The sun's gravitational force is very strong. If it were not, a planet would move in a straight line out into space forever. The sun's gravity pulls the planet toward the sun, which changes the straight line of direction into a curve. This keeps the planet moving in an orbit around the sun.

Because of the sun's gravitational pull, all the planets in our solar system orbit around it.

The sun is a huge ball of super-hot gas. Deep inside the sun, the temperature is hotter than the hottest furnace. The sun is so hot that it heats and lights all the planets in our solar system.

The orbits of the planets

Some planets orbit closer to the sun than others. And some are far away from the sun. The planets that are farthest from the sun are called the outer planets.

The planets that are closer to the sun are called the inner planets. The inner planets are close to each other as well as close to the sun. There are four inner planets:

Mercury
Venus
Earth
Mars

The inner planets have a hard, rocky surface. It is possible to land a spacecraft on planets that have a hard surface.

The five outer planets are not only farther from the sun, but they are also far apart from one another.

Four of them are much, much bigger than the inner planets. The four giant planets are:

Jupiter
Saturn
Uranus
Neptune

Mercury Venus Earth Mars

INNER PLANETS

Jupiter

Scientists believe that the surface of these huge planets is not solid. It is probably slushy.

The last planet discovered in our solar system is farthest away from the sun. It is Pluto. We don't know much about Pluto yet except that it is very, very cold.

Pluto is not like the other outer planets. And it is not like the inner planets, either. Pluto is a mystery.

This is how the nine planets compare in size with one another.

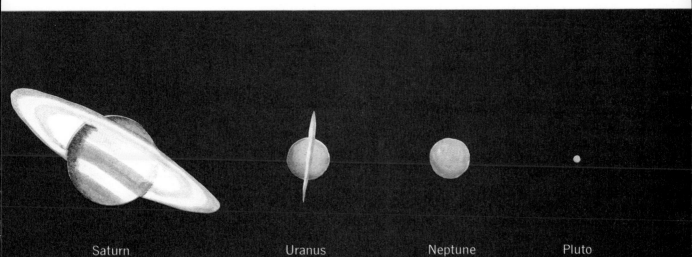

Saturn   Uranus   Neptune   Pluto

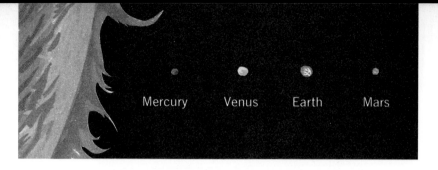

Mercury   Venus   Earth   Mars

THE INNER PLANETS

Earth

The two planets closest to the sun are Mercury and Venus. Next comes Earth. We know more about Earth than about any other planet.

Living things, as we know them, need sunlight, water, and certain gases. We know that Earth has what living things need. It has the right amount of sunlight. It has water — about three times as much water as land. And it has gases that plants and animals need to live.

Just above Earth is its atmosphere. Atmosphere is the air around an object in space. Not all objects in space have an atmosphere.

Earth does. Its atmosphere is made up mostly of nitrogen and oxygen. Dust particles float inside the atmosphere. So do clouds and microbes. (Microbes are living organisms so small you need a microscope to see them.) The clouds are water droplets that form rain.

Earth has a magnetic field all around it. The magnetic field begins inside Earth's core and goes out

This is how Earth looks from outer space.

way beyond the atmosphere. A magnetic field acts like a magnet.

Earth's atmosphere and the magnetic field above it block most of the deadly rays from the sun and other stars. Sometimes chunks of rock in space, called meteorites, attracted by Earth's gravity, enter our atmosphere. The atmosphere burns up most meteorites before they can hit Earth. Earth's atmosphere and magnetic field protect life on Earth.

Scientists believe there is probably life somewhere else in the universe. But they don't know where, yet.

The planet Earth spins around — rotates — once in 24 hours. With one 24-hour rotation, most of the planet has a night and a day.

A planet rotates as if there were a long rod through its center. But there is no rod. We make believe there is and call it an axis. The axis always points toward the North Star, tilting Earth as it orbits around the sun. Because of the tilt, parts of Earth are either closer to or farther from the sun at certain times of the year. These times are our seasons.

During winters at the North and South Poles, the nights last much longer than they do anywhere else on the planet. A winter night in the polar regions lasts all winter long. Summertime at the Poles is one very long day.

Earth has many kinds of climates. Temperatures on Earth can be as high as 60° Celsius (140° Fahrenheit). It gets that hot in some deserts. At the North and South Poles, it can be as cold as minus 90° Celsius (130° below zero Fahrenheit).

There may be some places on Earth where people may not be able to live. But some form of life is possible almost anywhere on Earth.

Rarely do meteorites pass through Earth's atmosphere. When one does hit the ground, it can make a wide, deep hole called a crater. This one is in Arizona and is the largest crater on Earth. It is 1,265 meters (4,150 feet) in diameter, and 175 meters (575 feet) deep.

Earth's partner

The moon is Earth's natural satellite. It takes the moon 27 days and 8 hours to circle Earth. Earth and moon orbit the sun together.

The moon's surface is a lot like Earth's. But the moon has no atmosphere, no magnetic field, no water, and no sign of life.

The moon, like Earth, is lit by the light of the sun. Now and then there are certain places on the moon that seem to glow with more light. Astronomers are not sure what causes this.

Earth and moon revolve around the sun in 365 days, plus part of another day. We make up for the part of a day by adding one extra day every four years. That year is called leap year and it has 366 days.

The surface of the moon, like Mercury and Mars, is dotted with craters made by meteorites. There is little or no atmosphere to stop them.

The picture on the left looks like the moon, but it's really Earth photographed from the moon.

Mercury

Mercury is the planet closest to the sun. It is also the smallest of all the known planets except for Pluto.

The nearby sun's glare makes it hard to see Mercury in the sky, even with a telescope.

More than three billion years ago, huge meteorites crashed into the planet. They left deep scars on its surface.

Mercury's atmosphere is much, much thinner than Earth's. There is also a very weak magnetic field around Mercury.

Mercury orbits the sun much faster than Earth does. But Mercury spins completely around on its axis much more slowly than Earth. While Mercury makes one spin, Earth has had 59 days and nights!

On Mercury, the days are terribly hot and the nights are terribly cold. There is no water. There is not much atmosphere. And the gases are not the kinds living things need. Scientists say there can't be any kind of life on Mercury.

This picture of Mercury was taken from space probe *Mariner 10*.

Venus

When you look up at the sky, the brightest objects you can see are the sun and the moon. The next brightest is Venus.

Venus is about the same size as Earth — just a little smaller. It is closer to Earth than any other planet. But it is very different from Earth.

Earth has lots of water, mostly in the form of oceans, rivers, and lakes. The only water we know of on Venus is in the form of water vapor. (Water vapor is a gas, which you cannot see.)

Earth turns on its axis in 24 hours. Venus turns on its axis very slowly. More than half a year passes on Earth before Venus has a new day.

Bright, yellowish clouds hide the surface of Venus. These clouds are made of sulfur particles and sulfuric acid.

Venus's clouds swirl around fast. Winds blow at about 350 kilometers (250 miles) an hour, stronger and wilder than any hurricane on Earth.

Two countries have explored Venus. The USSR has landed spacecraft on Venus. The United States has sent out probes that orbit the planet and can radar-map the surface. Its surface is rougher than Earth's and has many more craters.

Venus is nearly twice as far from the sun as Mercury, yet it is almost as hot as Mercury. Unlike Mercury, nights and days on Venus have about the same very high temperatures.

The reason for this is because Venus's atmosphere has carbon dioxide gas that stays all around the planet. It's like a blanket of smog that we sometimes get over some cities on Earth.

The sun's rays come through this atmosphere and heat the planet. The planet gives off heat rays, but those rays cannot pass back through the atmosphere to outer space. The heat is trapped under the blanket of carbon dioxide gas.

Something like this happens to a car parked in the sun with the windows shut. The inside gets much hotter than the outside because heat cannot escape.

On Venus, nothing we know of can live.

Mars

Mars is the inner planet farthest from the sun. It seems a lot like Earth. Nights and days on both planets take about the same time.

Though it's a bit colder on Mars, there are clouds and fog there. And it has volcanoes, lava fields, canyons, and cracks in its crust, like Earth.

Its North and South Poles also have ice caps.

Mars is called the Red Planet because its soil is red. Sand dunes, boulders, and rocks are part of the landscape. The white bar belongs to the spacecraft that landed on Mars and took the picture.

As Mars orbits, the ice cap closer to the sun shrinks because the sun's rays melt some of the ice.

About the same time each Mars year, part of the surface seems to change color. Mars seems to have seasons, as Earth does.

Jupiter

But there are differences between Mars and Earth. Mars has many moonlike craters, billions of years old. Its atmosphere is mostly carbon dioxide and much thinner than Earth's. Its sky is not blue, but creamy pink, because of red dust in the air.

Some geologists who study planets believe that once there used to be large, deep lakes on Mars under a much denser atmosphere. Now, dust storms sometimes cover the whole planet, and water on Mars is not liquid. It's in the form of vapor, ice clouds, or surface ice.

Mars has two satellites — tiny moons that re-volve around it.

Many scientists think some kind of life may be possible on Mars. So far, we have no proof of it. We hope to find answers with future space probes — and someday, even with a visit from Earth people.

Saturn Uranus Neptune Pluto

THE OUTER PLANETS

There is a very great distance between the inner and outer planets. This region is called the Asteroid Belt and large chunks of rock swarm around and around in it.

Except for Pluto, the outer planets are alike in a lot of ways.

They are much bigger than the inner planets.

They are made mostly of hydrogen and helium. The hydrogen and helium are in the form of gas in the planets' atmospheres. The outer planets have a lot of atmosphere.

The outermost part of these planets may be slushy. Below the surface, hydrogen and helium are in a liquid form. At the center is a rocky core.

Each of these huge planets has its own system of moons.

Rings around Saturn have been seen for many years. They are probably made mostly of water, ice, and other icy particles. Recently, rings have been discovered around two more giant planets— Jupiter and Uranus. Scientists expect to find rings around Neptune, too.

PLANETS OF OUR SOLAR SYSTEM	How far from the sun (average distance)	How long to make one spin on its axis
Mercury	58 million kilometers (36 million miles)	59 Earth days
Venus	108 million kilometers (67 million miles)	243 Earth days
Earth	150 million kilometers (93 million miles)	24 Earth hours
Mars	228 million kilometers (142 million miles)	24½ Earth hours
Asteroid Belt	550 million kilometers (341 million miles)	
Jupiter	778 million kilometers (483 million miles)	Just less than 10 Earth hours
Saturn	1,427 million kilometers (886 million miles)	10¼ Earth hours
Uranus	3 billion kilometers (2 billion miles)	About 17 Earth hour
Neptune	4½ billion kilometers (3 billion miles)	About 18 Earth hour
Pluto	6 billion kilometers (3½ billion miles) See footnote on page 36.	7 Earth days

* If you went from one side of a planet, through the center to the other side, that would be the diameter.

How long to orbit once around the sun	Diameter*	Number of satellites
38 Earth days	4,900 kilometers (3,000 miles)	None
7½ Earth months	12,100 kilometers (7,500 miles)	None
1 Earth year	12,800 kilometers (7,900 miles)	1
23 Earth months	6,800 kilometers (4,200 miles)	2
12 Earth years	142,800 kilometers (89,000 miles)	17 — may be more
29½ Earth years	120,000 kilometers (75,000 miles)	22 — may be more
84 Earth years	51,800 kilometers (32,000 miles)	15 — may be more
165 Earth years	49,500 kilometers (31,000 miles)	6 — may be more
250 Earth years	2,200 kilometers (1,400 miles)	1

Jupiter

Jupiter, the first of the outer planets, is the largest of all the planets. Jupiter is so far away from Earth that it was hard to learn much about it with only telescopes.

In 1977, *Voyagers 1* and *2* — United States space probes — were sent off into space from Earth. They sped through space all the way to Jupiter and sent back a lot of new information.

Jupiter's outer atmosphere is very cold. But inside the planet, it gets hotter and hotter closer to the center.

Scientists do not think life exists on Jupiter.

Jupiter spins fast on its axis. But this giant planet takes a long time to go around the sun. One Jupiter year is as long as 12 Earth years.

Astronomers expect the new information about Jupiter's moons to help explain how our solar system began, how it changed, and how Earth came to be the way it is.

Several pictures are made into one to show Jupiter and its four biggest moons. Jupiter's rings are too thin to be seen in this photograph. Can you see the planet's belts and zones, its Great Red Spot, and the smaller white spots? The moon in the bottom corner looks bigger than Jupiter because it is closer to the camera, but it really is smaller.

Fast-moving clouds whirl around Jupiter. They form a pattern of wide bands called zones and narrow bands called belts.

In one of the zones is a tremendous oval called the Great Red Spot. It is three times as big as Earth. Most scientists are not sure what the Great Red Spot really is. Some scientists think it may be a giant hurricane.

Jupiter has rings. There is also a magnetic field around Jupiter 10,000 times more powerful than Earth's. And Jupiter, the super planet, has super lightning bolts!

For hundreds of years, people could see four of Jupiter's moons through telescopes. Now we know Jupiter has at least 17 moons. Jupiter's mass is much greater than all the other planets together. Remember, greater mass means greater gravity. That's probably why Jupiter has so many satellites which keep revolving around this planet with its tremendous gravitational pull. They orbit Jupiter as Jupiter orbits the sun.

The Great Red Spot looks like a big red eye.
Swirling clouds keep moving all around it.

Saturn

Beautiful Saturn, with its bright rings, is the second largest planet in our solar system. Saturn is almost 10 times bigger than Earth.

Saturn is much, much farther from the sun than Earth. It is very cold out there! And it takes almost 30 of our years for Saturn to go once around the sun.

Like the other very big planets, Saturn is mostly hydrogen and helium.

From far away, Saturn looks yellowish. But close-up photographs taken from the two *Voyager* space probes show it has bands of different colors — pale yellow, golden brown, and reddish brown.

Saturn has many moons. Twenty-two have been discovered already. The moon named Titan, one of the largest in the solar system, has a lot of atmosphere.

Maybe Titan's atmosphere, like that around Venus, has kept heat from escaping into space. Maybe Titan's atmosphere and surface have stayed warm over billions of years. And maybe here we may find some form of life.

Here is Saturn and its famous rings. Scientists believe rings form when a satellite gets too close to the mother planet. The planet's gravity pulls the satellite apart. Particles of the satellite form rings that circle the planet.

Uranus

All the planets described so far have been known for a long, long time. Uranus was discovered only about 200 years ago by a scientist looking through a telescope.

Uranus is the third of the four big outer planets. It is a small giant — fuzzy and blue — only four times bigger than Earth. It has at least 15 moons.

The orbit of Uranus is very, very far from the sun. The planet is tipped over so that it rotates like a top spinning almost on its side. Sunlight and darkness at the North Pole of Uranus each lasts 42 Earth years.

Life on Uranus is not likely.

Uranus also has rings, but they are narrow, dark, and hard to see. They were discovered while astronomers watched Uranus come close to a star. The star began to flicker before and after Uranus passed in front of it. Astronomers realized the flickering was due to rings that partly blocked the star's light for a few moments. When *Voyager 2* passed Uranus in 1986, it showed a close-up of the planet's rings.

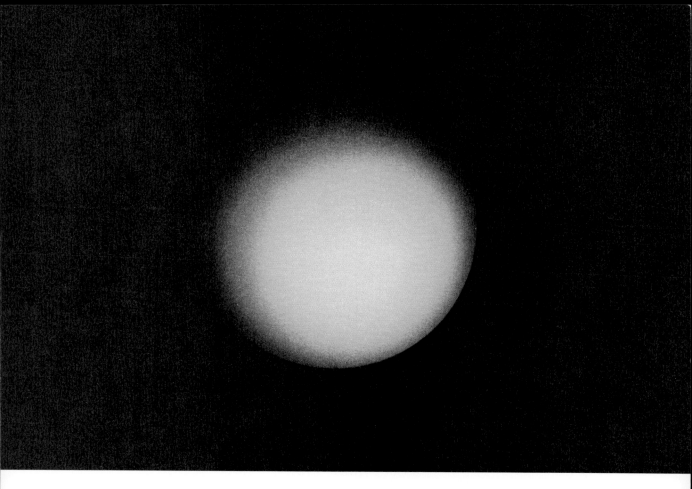

This photograph of Uranus was taken from *Voyager 2* in January 1986. It shows the planet as the human eye would see it from the spacecraft — 9.1 million kilometers (5.7 million miles) away.

When scientists studied Uranus, they found that its orbit was slightly different from what they thought it would be. They thought the difference might be due to the gravitational pull of another planet. So they looked for another planet. They discovered two — Neptune and Pluto.

Neptune

Of the four giant planets, Neptune is farthest away from the sun. It is a very cold planet.

Neptune is a little smaller than Uranus.

It takes a little less time than Earth to rotate once. But it takes 165 Earth years for Neptune to make one orbit around the sun.

Neptune has three known satellites.

Scientists believe that two rings circle Neptune. *Voyager 2* is expected to pass near Neptune in 1989. Then we should have more exact information.

Pluto

Pluto is a puzzle. It is farthest away from the sun* but it is not a giant planet. Some scientists think this planet once may have been a satellite of Neptune. If that is so, Pluto may have been pulled away by the gravity of still another planet — a planet not yet discovered.

Other scientists believe that Pluto and its very close moon, Charon, are really a double planet sharing the same atmosphere. This would be the only double planet in our solar system.

* Because of the way Pluto orbits, there is a time when Neptune is farther from the sun than Pluto. That is what is happening now. It happens every 248 years. By 1999, Pluto will again be the farthest planet from the sun.

THE STARS

How the universe began

Many scientists believe that between 10 and 20 billion years ago, there was a tremendous explosion. It occurred everywhere in the universe. It is called "The Big Bang."

When this happened, matter was scattered throughout the universe. Small bunches of matter made up such bodies as dust particles, gases, asteroids, meteors, and comets. Much greater amounts of matter bunched together to form planets. Far greater amounts bunched close together and became stars.

One of the stars became the sun, the center of our solar system in the Milky Way galaxy.

The Milky Way is only one of billions of galaxies in the universe. Scientists today are discovering that the universe is bigger than anyone before ever imagined. Galaxies bunch together making super clusters in what may be an even greater system.

We can photograph at least a billion galaxies with our powerful telescopes. Some are nearer to us than others. But when we talk about outer space, "near" means billions of kilometers away!

The Milky Way galaxy is 100,000 light-years in diameter. Our solar system is two thirds of the way between the center and edge of the galaxy.

This is the Andromeda galaxy. Many galaxies have a spiral shape like this one.

Today, we can get information about objects so far out in space that it takes many, many years for their light to reach us. When we look at a blinking star that is light-years away, we are seeing something that started a very long time ago.

As we look out in space, we look back in time. Scientists, called astrophysicists, know much more now about the different stages of objects that form deep in space. Gradually, we understand better how stars are born, what happens to them while they are stars, and what becomes of them when they die.

The life of a star

What is a star made of? How is it born? Why does it shine? Will it live forever? These are questions people have been asking for ages.

Stars are huge, very, very hot balls of gas that shine brightly. How did they get that way?

All matter, from the tiniest microscopic particle to the biggest galaxy, starts with atoms.

Oxygen is an element made up of oxygen atoms. Hydrogen is an element made up of hydrogen atoms. Atoms combine to make different molecules. For example, when oxygen and hydrogen come

The nucleus of an atom contains protons and neutrons. Tiny lightweight electrons zip around the nucleus, as shown in this drawing of an atom. The number of protons in the nucleus of an atom determines the type of element it is.

together, they form a molecule we can't live without—water. Elements, alone or combined with other elements, make up all the matter that exists.

Look around you. Whatever you see is made up of elements — rocks, rain, the air we breathe. We are made up of certain elements. So are the stars.

The simplest and lightest element is hydrogen gas. Enormous clouds of hydrogen gas and dust particles form in space. Gravity draws the dust and gas close together forming a huge clump, or mass.

As more and more matter is added to the mass, its gravity increases. This pushes the atoms of hydrogen gas closer and closer together. The mass begins to contract, or get smaller. It also gets denser and hotter. The center is hottest of all because the atoms are being squeezed together. The heat creates tremendous energy. Energy is the power necessary to make things happen.

Finally, the crowding of the atoms, the heat, and the violent energy forces the hydrogen atoms to combine. This makes a new and heavier element called helium. The change of hydrogen gas to helium gas is called thermonuclear fusion. When this happens a star is born.

Throughout a star's life, thermonuclear fusion goes on in its core, creating enormous energy. That energy becomes light and heat. It makes the star shine. The same kind of energy from our shining star, the sun, travels billions of kilometers to reach us here on Earth.

Our sun is a medium-sized star that is medium bright. There are others like it. The universe has stars that are much larger and much smaller than our sun.

The new star will shine in the heavens for billions of years. It will stay that way until all its hydrogen gas has changed to helium.

The death of a star

When a star has finally turned all its hydrogen into helium it is nearing the end of its life. Scientists believe that the amount of mass left in the dead star determines what will become of it.

Because our sun is of average size, astronomers use it to measure other stars. At the end of its life, a star with the same amount of mass as our sun will shrink to about the size of Earth. That's a million times smaller!

Sirius, the brightest-looking star in the sky, is shown here with its companion — a tiny white dwarf known as Sirius B. If you could take a teaspoonful of a white dwarf's tightly packed mass, it would weigh thousands of kilograms — as much as a truckload of bricks.

Matter gets packed so tightly that the force of gravity pulls the star into itself. The star gets so hot it turns white. This small dead star is called a *white dwarf.*

When an even bigger star — a giant star — uses up all its energy, it collapses even more than a white dwarf. Its mass and gravity are much greater. No space is left between the atoms. Electrons and protons inside the atoms are pushed together. They become neutrons and the giant star shrinks to a very small size. It is called a *neutron star* and is usually only a few kilometers in diameter. But its mass is so great that a tiny bit of neutron star — less than a teaspoonful — would weigh about half a trillion kilograms. That's as much as a long freight train loaded with bricks!

Sometimes, when a giant star collapses, particles called neutrinos are forced out of the atoms. As the neutrinos burst forth from the dying star, the star shines more brightly than any other object in the galaxy. It looks like an enormous sparkler. This is a *supernova*.

When the amount of mass left in a dying star is three or more times the mass of the sun, something very mysterious happens. A star this massive shrinks much faster than the white dwarf and the neutron star. Its force of gravity is very great. Nothing can escape it — not even light, which moves faster than anything else in the universe. This star becomes a *black hole*.

Many astrophysicists believe that there are black holes at the center of most galaxies, including our Milky Way. Although that may be so, our solar system is too far removed from the black hole for us to be influenced by its pull of gravity.

A supernova at the time of its explosion can be as bright as a whole galaxy. This one was seen by a Chinese astronomer in the year 1054.

WHAT NEXT?

Because of tremendous advances in technology, scientists believe we are just beginning a new age of astronomy.

Computers can tell us quickly how, when, and why certain events will happen. Large groups of

antennae gather data from outer space. Observatories are equipped to scan the skies day and night. Sensors on telescopes can detect radiations that were invisible before.

Many of these radiations cannot pass through Earth's atmosphere. But we have the space shuttle that takes us out of Earth's gravitational pull and beyond Earth's atmosphere.

The shuttle can carry instruments into space and launch them as satellites. From there, they send back to Earth information we could never get before. They are like windows on the world.

Someday we may build a station in space that will give us an even greater chance to learn about the universe.

Astronomers and astrophysicists expect to get clearer answers to some big questions: How exactly did the world begin, and will it go on forever?

Perhaps you will become a scientist — one who may discover even more wondrous things about the planets, the stars, and the universe.

This is one of the U.S. space shuttles. It can take off like a rocket, orbit around Earth, change course in space, return to Earth, land like a glider, and be used over and over again.

Photo credits

The publisher is grateful for permission
to use the following photographs:

AP/Wide World
Pages 19, 35, 38

Freelance Photographers Guild
Pages 4-5

Hale Observatories
Page 45

Lick Observatory/University of California at Santa Cruz
Page 43

NASA
Front cover and pages 8, 13, 17, 20, 22-23, 29, 31, 33, 46

National Optical Astronomy Observatory
Page 39

University of Chicago
Page 40

Yerkes Observatory/University of Chicago
Page 14

Illustrations by Ted Hanke